THE GREATEST LIE
The Untold Truth

BY JAMIE PHILLIPS

Dorrance Publishing Co
585 Alpha Drive
Suite 103
Pittsburgh, PA 15238
Visit our website at *www.dorrancebookstore.com*

ISBN: 978-1-6393-7213-3
eISBN: 978-1-6393-7892-0

The Untold Truth

WITHIN THIS TEXT LIES THE TRUTH BEHIND THE DEMOCRATIC party, which I will demonstrate. Though nothing but facts will tell the unbridled truth about the Democrats, I will show the similarities between today's Democrats and 1930s Nazi regime.

It all starts with the role of the media. The media of the past is the same as present day. Pushing an agenda and convincing the population that what is said is right and everyone else is wrong. This is a brainwashing technique, used since man spoke his first words thousands of years ago. The key to ruling a country is fear through the media. If you hear something repeated over and over eventually it becomes your truth. Although times have changed since 1930-45, the political climate has not.

The journalists are the ones that carry the blame by glamorizing violence, the condemnation of those who are in opposition to their ideas. Villainization of good people and the promotion of the bad. When all or most of the media believe one way, it reinforces its viewers' ideology and vilifies opposing views. This is what causes division in countries. The way to counter this is open discussion and debates to come to an intelligent and well-thought-out remedy for any problem.

I will also show that not only did the Democrats support slavery, start the KKK, and support the Jim Crow movement, but I will show that Joe Biden was called out during the primaries by his now VP that he is a racist.

We hold these truths to be self-evident, that all men are created equal, that they are endowed by their creator with certain unalienable rights. That among these are life, liberty and the pursuit of happiness. – Declaration of Independence

1889 Austria, Adolph Hitler was born to Austrian-Bavarian parents. As a young adult he joined the Bavarian Army and was an infantryman for a couple years. Then transferred to the 16th Regiment, known as the list regiment, where he spent the rest of his military time.

In 1918 he left the service as a postman and never made the rank past private. The unambitious Hitler now on the streets of Nuremberg, wandering and just looking around, saw all the Jewish businesses flourishing. He thought that the German people should have that wealth. He thought the Jewish people with their long hair and beards were dirty and didn't deserve the money they were earning.

Hitler walked for a bit before he found a pub and went in. He wasn't a drinker, he ordered a coffee and sat down. As he sat there listening to the crowd of Germans complaining about the Jews, he had decided that enough was enough. At this point he grabbed a stool, stood on it, and gave the best speech the German men had ever heard. Hitler must have been an excellent speaker, because he caught the attention of a journalist, Erin Einhardt, who was sitting in the corner drinking and writing. Einhardt approached Hitler and asked him to walk for a bit.

Einhardt complimented Hitler on his ability to speak publicly and asked Hitler to come to his apartment. Hitler complied, when they entered

Einhardt's apartment, he gave Hitler a suit, hat, and overcoat and told him to get dressed in these. After Hitler was better dressed, Einhardt took Hitler into the street. They walked and spoke to everyone that would listen, this man is the next leader of Germany.

Hitler had an epiphany and said he wanted to do something more. Einhardt introduced Hitler to Josef Goebbels, who at the time was in charge of a little-known political party called the Nazi party. Goebbels liked Hitler and soon after recruited him. After a few years, Hitler climbed through the ranks of the party. He started publicly speaking again. By that act of speaking he alone started growing the Nazi party by recruiting people through his speeches.

The party grew by great numbers and was starting to become a formidable political force. Hitler wanted more, he and Rudolph Hess decided to create a coup d'état and take control of the country by force. Hitler and Hess were arrested and sentenced to 5 years. Hitler only ended up doing 18 months. After his release from jail, Hitler decided to run for office knowing that trying to take it by force was a moot idea. Hitler gave his speeches and soon won the chancellorship. After a year as chancellor he wanted the entire country. His problem was the president of Germany at the time, Hindenburg.

Hindenburg was a fair leader and Hitler wanted the top spot. After 2 years Hindenburg died. Hitler then had an easy transition into the seat of power. Hitler decided to control the country. Not knowing where to begin, he decided to start with the media. He understood that the media would get his word out to the people.

The media of the time was radio and newspapers. The fundamental task of the media has always been to bring the news of the day. Hitler tasked Josef Goebbels with media and propaganda. News by radio only reached half of the population. Hitler then had Goebbels make new radio towers and 7 million radios. This way Hitler could have his voice heard in every home in Germany. After all homes had one, Hitler had mandated that all citizens listen to him for one hour each day. This way everyone could hear him twice a day.

Hitler, being an excellent public speaker, would now have the ability to tell the German people how grand and advantageous his ideas were and how they would be good for Germany. All the radio stations and newspapers complied with Hitler, whether out of fear of retribution or love of the Fuhrer is still unclear. By hearing Hitler all the time the people believed him and eventually loved him.

November 27, 1933, there was a fire in the Nazi headquarters building. Hitler went on the radio and told the people that the communists were trying to take the country and ruin the Nazi party. He got the parliament together that next day. He asked them to vote on a bill. This bill was the REISCHTAG Fire Decree. This decree stated that the citizens may lose a few freedoms for security. It passed, and now Hitler had total control of the German people without them knowing. Slowly Hitler took more and more rights from the people. By controlling the media he had inadvertently taken their right to speak freely. He went on the radio, asking people to surrender their guns. He understood that an armed population had the ability to unseat him. He left the people their guns used for hunting. Next was the right to privacy. At this point the S.A. and S.S. could come to a person's house and use it or contents therein it, if it was deemed necessary.

As the war pressed on Hitler needed more fighting men on the frontline. Hitler tasked Heinrik Himler with figuring this problem out. Himler came up with an idea but it was radical. Hitler heard this and thought it was brilliant. Then told Himler to begin.

Heinrik Himler started what was known as the junior ranks, these ranks were children as young as ten. These young boys after training were given a few tasks. Being part of the S.A. they would be in the streets. One of their tasks was to make lists of people who talked badly of the Fuhrer or the Nazi party. Those people would be rounded up later. The other task was to throw rocks through the windows of Jewish businesses and paint the building with "Don't buy from Jews" and march down the streets with signs of the same message. A while later, Hitler had the S.S. look these people up on these lists and his words were, "Round them up and punish them accordingly."

Alexandria Ocasio-Cortez made such lists and has made the same statement in Congress and is now calling for the removal or arrest of all Republicans that are close to Donald Trump, i.e. Sen. Matriomo, Sen. Cruz. etc.. Since then the list has grown and is now calling for all Trump supporters to be harassed in public and shamed. This is the very thing that divides a country. This is also a Nazi tactic that proved useful to get the people in line with the Nazi program.

Hitler had two different types of speeches. One was of unity and to bring Germany back better and stronger. The second speech was if we don't do something about the problem (Jews) we are all going to die.

Joe Biden has those two same speeches but the second is the virus, which is what Hitler referred to the Jews as.

PRESENT DAY

THE DEMOCRATS HAVE ACTUALLY DONE OR ARE DOING EVERYTHING that Hitler did to date. They own 90% of the media. On Joe Biden's website he has it that online sales of guns, gun parts, and accessories are going to be illegal. He is also having Beto O'Rourke head up a committee, to take guns out of the hands of the people. The media is telling people on the right to shut up, and telling their viewers everything is gonna be alright. The Second Amendment states that a well-regulated militia being necessary to the security of a free state and it is the right of the people to keep and bear arms shall not be infringed.

They want to take what they refer to as assault weapons, what exactly is an assault weapon? Is it one that looks scary or is it all guns? I was in Iraq from 03-05, we used shotguns, pistols, M4 rifles. and long-range hunting rifles as well as M14s. I believe it means any gun that shoots a bullet. It is the beginning of a socialistic society run by a tyrannical and totalitarian government. These are the times that try men's souls.

They are using the COVID virus as a catalyst the same way Hitler used REICHSTAG. With the politics in the United States right now in confusion, this country has no sense of itself from top to bottom. People are accepting this as normal, instead of speaking out. Biden wants a 4-week lockdown and 100 more days of wearing a mask. The mask isn't the issue, it's the loss of personal freedoms. Carrying a medical card saying you have been vaccinated is a HIPAA violation and yet, here we are.

Hitler had Mussolini, Biden has Xi Jing Ping. During the conflict in Eastern Europe at the time Hitler had asked Mussolini to help with his war efforts. Since Hitler had the largest military, he gave aid, mobile military bases and troops so the S.S. would be closer to support.

China has recently been buying farms all over Oklahoma, for up to three times the value. The reason is unclear at this point in time. They also put military bases in the Bahamas, including Naval and ground forces. The United States uses its home-based military as a kind of buffer between the government and civilians. This way any civil unrest or disobedience can be handled immediately. An overwhelming force of Chinese national military could possibly take a lot of real estate in a short period of time. The results would be devastating. We know Joe Biden is pro-Chinese as well as Bloomberg and all of the alphabet news channels, and most celebrity figures. Charles Lindberg was a Nazi sympathizer saying that they are not bad people. He was the media celebrity of the day, kind of like any celebrity today. He also said they were not socialists and were not killing people. Joe Biden has said the same of the Chinese. A media commentator I listen to said a few weeks back that the Chinese were rounding up the people of Hong Kong and putting them on busses heading for re-education camps. My belief is that China wants to take us down from the inside.

Joe Biden has a son, Hunter, who is now under an active investigation for not paying taxes and money laundering from the country of China. The FBI is seeing if Joe had anything to do with it. Apparently Joe, his brother Frank and Hunter had split the money and are now denying it. The circumstances surrounding the money are sketchy at best. Hunter had a laptop that ended up in the hands of Rudy Giuliani and at present is in the custody of the FBI. Bobulinski, a former friend of the Biden family, has come forward with evidence of Hunter and Joe Biden that implicates both of them with colluding with the Chinese government. Mr. Bobulinski also confirmed that Joe used his position as vice president to have a Ukrainian prosecutor fired from his position for having Hunter under investigation. When the prime minister said no, Joe Biden told him if he didn't fire the prosecutor Joe would not release the aid money to Ukraine. The prosecutor was fired directly. Joe purposely withheld aid money from a country in need that the American people wanted to help for his own personal gain.

This would explain the military presence so close to the United States and the Oklahoma property. Saying something to the civic leaders doesn't help. Number one, they won't look to see if it's true and just think you are crazy or they do look at it and tell you it's not true and tell you to shut up about it. All government leaders lie about everything as long as it helps them personally or politically.

During the summer of 2020 riots all over the country broke out. The first was Minneapolis. 400 million dollars in damage and a number of civilian deaths. One such death was David Dorn. A retired police officer working security at a store. Antifa and BLM broke the doors down and started looting, Mr. Dorn trying to stop the anarchy was killed. Then the rest of the riots and autonomous zones in Seattle, Portland, Chicago and St. Louis. More recently was the siege at the Capitol. Where an officer died of his injuries and a woman was shot by Capitol police. The woman, Lieutenant Babbit, an Air Force intel officer. She was shot in the neck dying from her wounds minutes later. The Democrats were quick to blame Donald Trump for this woman and the officer's death. It was said that Donald Trump incited this by telling supporters to do it. The speech he gave said to peacefully and patriotically protest. This paved the way for an impeachment. Donald Trump has denied all allegations of his complicity in this heinous act. He has since denounced this and said the perpetrators should be held accountable and jailed. That did not stop the Democrats from saying it was his fault and he should be jailed.

Although Donald Trump has spoken out about this riot and the riots during the summer, he was told by Democrats, as we were, that the summer riots were peaceful protests. Not to call in the federal officers under the Insurrection Act. Federal officers were called to protect federal buildings during this time and President Trump was called all sorts of names for not condoning riots led by domestic terror groups such as BLM and ANTIFA.

The people that we heard nothing from during these riots that cost American lives 300 civilians, 275 police officers and 400 million dollars in damage. Where was Joe Biden and Kamala Harris? Kamala Harris actually said there should be more protests like this and called on the rich Democrats to bail rioters out of jail. Mike Bloomberg was one of these individuals. This is why the Second Amendment is so vital to our freedom. The 1st, 2nd and 4th amendments are what keep this country from becoming a communist nation that has a government that can do as it pleases. This is why Congress needs to be put in check.

To keep Congress from getting out of hand ever again I have suggestions. First we give them a salary cap. Right now they can get 2 raises a year and for Congress alone it's over 8 million dollars a year in taxpayer money and make it so they can't get over $150,000 a year. If you're in Congress and getting rich you are a criminal. Then we need to have the taxpayers stop paying for Congressmen and women's medical, they should have a plan they pay for, just like everyone else in America they have a job. We do not need to pay for their kids' college loans, we have to pay our children's, they should have to. Make lobbying illegal, if big companies need something they need to ask for it, not pay someone in Congress millions to make sure that their company gets what they want in regulations or tax cuts.

The First Amendment says that the people have the right to free speech. As of late I can say that isn't true. Donald Trump was banned from Twitter, Facebook, etc. The big tech companies took his right of free speech. When the tech giants couldn't shut him down on Parler they got rid of the entire platform and disenfranchised an entire group of people. Taking their right to free speech. This I believe is an attack on my First Amendment rights. Maybe some people don't want him on social media but it is his right to be heard and my right to hear what he has to say. If they can do that to a sitting president it will not be long before it comes to all of us. Our rights under the Constitution are fading rapidly because of Democrat ideology and no one person's voice should be suppressed, ever.

Next is our Fourth Amendment, and most important. The Fourth Amendment is about illegal search and seizure and the reasonable expectation of privacy. Hitler took his people's right of this and the S.S. went into people's homes without consent. If we lose this right the government will be able to come into our homes and take what they please. Including guns and that is where we lose the Second Amendment. The loss of the First Amendment is just the beginning.

This is how Hitler had a hold on the people of Germany and we the people cannot let this happen. If it does I fear a civil war may ensue. The founding fathers started this country under the ideology that all men are created equal and no man should be kept under the thumb of a tyrannical system. In the Declaration of Independence it says, "Through a long train of abuses and usurpations chasing invariably the same object, it evinces a design to reduce them to absolute despotism, it is our right, it is our duty to throw off such government and place new guards for future securities." This means that if we are in a tyrannical system we need to change it because the government won't if they believe the populous is comfortable where they are.

Through history the Democratic ideology has been at the forefront of every major tragedy. They supported slavery, Abraham Lincoln was the Republican who in 1863 wrote the Emancipation Proclamation to free slaves and was killed by a southern Democrat, John W. Booth. The southern Democrats were against this because not only would they lose their workforce but they would lose money they spent on the slaves themselves. No Democrat has ever allowed shortcomings in the bank.

Shortly after Lincoln was assassinated, the Democrats wanted revenge on the slaves that were free and not indentured to them. Here is where the lynch mobs started but the southern Democrats didn't have a name, until in 1866 the Ku Klux Klan was born. The KKK ran from 1866-1870, then from 1915 to present.

From 1877 to 1964 the Jim Crow movement was born. Democrats supported this movement. Joe Biden has been cited saying that he didn't want his kids growing up in a social jungle. During the presidential primaries Kamala Harris called him out on it saying she was that little girl Joe didn't want on the bus. Joe Biden also gave a eulogy at Robert Byrd's funeral. Byrd was high up in the KKK. Biden never renounced it or the KKK.

On January 11, 2021, Joe Biden had a press conference and told the American People he was going to help rebuild small businesses. Which normally would be a good thing. The problem is, he said he would help rebuild black, Asian, and Latino businesses. The one word that was left out of that speech was Caucasian. This by any account is a racist statement. Nancy Pelosi also had a presser where she stated that you are choosing your "whiteness" over democracy.

Hitler was racist as well, a well-known anti-Semite and creator of the most horrific acts in history and was a Democrat socialist. During the holocaust 11 million Jews were murdered by Hitler between 1933-1946. It was genocide.

Bernie Sanders, A.O.C. and the squad are also Democrat socialists who would love to bring socialism to the forefront of this country. A.O.C. said President Trump should be severely punished more than just impeachment. His supporters should be held accountable as well. For what is still unclear.

Ronald Reagan said if socialism comes to the United States it will come in the name of liberalism. No truer words have been spoken out loud in a long time.

As I sit here and rant, I am compelled to speak of another serious matter, defunding the police. Joe Biden says not to defund but reallocate their money for training social workers to go with them. Taking money from the police no matter how you look at it is defunding them, it's just a different name. Hitler defunded the police in 1930. He kept a small unit of the Polizei and got rid of the police. He used the young kids, and the other brown shirts and put them in their place. The reason was to reallocate money for the people he meant to rule under the guise of socialism. The police need to be celebrated not chastised for how a few act, although I do understand that there are some good and some not. Without police presence the United States would fall into chaos and anarchy and the criminals would totally take over.

Now if I haven't convinced you that the left side of the aisle needs some reform then I never will. Back in the 1970-80s they were the workers' party. Sadly since then they have spiraled into a chasm of hate and darkness. Hitler's party was actually called the National Socialist German Workers Party. The Democrats would have you believe that they are what is good for the country. Just as Hitler did with Germany.

The greatest lie ever told was when the devil convinced man that he didn't exist.

My entire childhood my parents told me that if you don't pay attention to history you are doomed to repeat it. In our society we have people in positions of power, and are cancelling our history. Statues being pulled down, and books being banned. Our rights are a part of our history, amendments and civil liberties. As I have explained we are now reaping what we sow. By repeating the history we fought so hard as a country to fix, the problems of the past. If our history disappears we won't have a guideline to show us what not to do. The mistakes from the past will inevitably come back to haunt our future.

This whole election fraud ordeal has happened in the past a few times, all

Democrat orchestrated. The 1800s was a bad time for elections and so is the early 21st century, apparently.

What has transpired during this election is an abuse of power by the left, and I believe gross negligence by the right. The left flooded the system with fake ballots, illegals voting and dead people posting their votes through. In two states there were more votes than registered voters, voting machines flipping votes. Since the Supreme Court didn't want to see the evidence, the signed affidavits, didn't want to hear from the scholars who have said the math doesn't work out or even looking at the actual numbers from the state legislature. When it went before the Senate, Mike Pence had it within his purview to send electors back to the state legislatures and make them do their jobs. This causes a severe lack of trust in elections and government.

It is not about Donald Trump losing, this is about the fairness of elections and the disenfranchising of 74 million Americans. If there are that many people thinking that this election was fraudulent, then the evidence should have at least been looked at. This was left to the Congress, which in my opinion has been corrupted by either money or threats of violence. Kelly Loeffler said in front of Congress, "In light of today's actions, I was going to vote against electors but now am forced to decline to do so." She got spooked by something other than the siege on the Capitol building. Ironically enough she, by saying that is now not on A.O.C.'s list of Republicans who she says need punishment.

Thomas Jefferson said, "It is the great parent of science and of virtue and that a nation will be great in both, always in proportion as long as it is free."

Freedom of the press doesn't mean you can say whatever you want and expect it to be true or what you believe is true. It means that a free press won't be subject to scrutiny, because of its validity. Lying to the people is morally and journalistically wrong. That is the way Hitler took control. Freedom of the press should always be something we adhere to as a nation. It also should be fair and honest and not opinionated. The American people deserve the truth.

In the Declaration of Independence and in the U.S. Constitution, it states that the people that govern are ruled by the governed. This just means that WE THE PEOPLE is literal. We make the rules and set precedence not the House of Representatives or Senate or even the president themselves. We as a free people have forgotten who is in charge. WE ARE! We need to get back to being a great country.

Teaching our children how to love their country, by saying the Pledge of Allegiance and have a belief in God. When a child says the pledge every morning and learns what it means, then that child will have a greater respect for people, the law and government. It gives that child something to believe in, something that they are a part of something wonderful and can be free. A great many men and women died under the belief that this country was worth it and their children and grandchildren would have a better America to live in than the generation before.

Some came home under the flag in which so many seek to destroy and disrespect, by kneeling or sitting down during sport functions. People fought and died for the freedom they have to do that, but just because you have the right to do certain things doesn't necessarily mean that you should. There is a time and place for everything, in a sports arena probably isn't that place. If you've got a problem go see the mayor or governor or a representative. There are alternatives to get your points across. Teaching children these acts of disrespect to our flag, our anthem and our founding fathers, and our country raises entitled children who grow up to believe that they can get the results they are looking for if they whine long enough. Teach them how to use the system to get their point across and raise kids to be respectful and knowledgeable adults.

If history teaches us anything, it tells us how to act how to behave in a civilized society and right from wrong. We as a nation have to come together, stop the divisive thinking and this critical theory garbage and stop pushing your ideologies on people. We need to get back to the fundamentals and realize this nation first without regard for skin color or sexual orientation. Or any other thing that may offend. I don't get offended because lately I have noticed I drink coffee stronger than most people's feelings. So if anything within these pages offends you just take solace in the fact that I DON'T CARE!

We as a nation have gone out of our way to appease the younger generation and other countries, it's about time we stop with the nonsense. Let men be masculine and women feminine and let everyone else do their own thing. As a veteran and have been in multiple countries I have seen what happens when a communist or socialist idea turns into reality. If what we see happening now continues I am afraid of what comes next. The persecution of people of religion. We have already seen the abhorrent behavior of certain ethnic groups going after people of a faith. NYC 2019: 4 black youths beat two Jewish men in the streets, Bill DeBlasio said nothing, one white cop and one Asian cop in NYC shot and killed, DeBlasio says nothing. When will these leaders be leaders instead of turning their heads because of skin color, wrong is wrong regardless of your skin color, sexual orientation, or political viewpoint. This is happening all over our great nation. We have black people telling white people to get on their knees in the street and ask for forgiveness for being white or that their ancestors were slave owners. Kamala Harris' great-grandfather owned slaves in the Bahamas, her grandfather wrote a book about it. Oprah Winfrey on television talking about white privilege and our whiteness, and trying to make white people feel bad about things they were never involved in. This is what is causing racial divide, not the police. The job of a police officer is hard enough, and then people who break the law all of a sudden call cops racist because they were arrested and then they are released because of systemic racism. All of these people only know half-truths or a small part of the story and turn it into some kind of racial conspiracy that gets turned around by the media into some kind of systemic problem. In reality it's an individual ideology and not a widespread systemic problem.

1934: an oil tycoon named William R. Davis saw the war breaking out and knew he had an opportunity to make a lot of money by selling oil to Germany. It would have been treason to sell any commodity to an enemy of America. To get around this he took his oil to Mexico and sold it to Germany from there. This was colluding with the enemy. When he got his oil to the shores of Germany, the British Navy would not let him through. Losing a lot of money, he asked Franklin Roosevelt for an audience FDR denied at that time. Two weeks after Poland was invaded FDR called Davis to the White House. Davis, trying to make an ally of FDR, asked if he could try to broker a peace treaty with Germany. He knew if he talked to the Germans he could figure out how to get his oil there and stop the hemorrhaging money. FDR told Davis that he was not to try to make this deal with his name attached to it. When Davis arrived in Germany he spoke with a colonel in the SS for about five hours. The colonel asked him why he was there, he told him that he was there on behalf of the president. The colonel told Davis he would bring it to the Fuhrer if he helped Germany unseat the president, he agreed. Germany said they would be in touch. At home Davis recruited the help of a man in the president's cabinet named John Lewis, secretary of finance. The ROGGE Report states that Germany had financed this coup d'état. They had given Davis and Lewis 5 million dollars to get this done. This happened during a U.S. Presidential election. So Davis and Lewis knew that FDR was losing support so they gave money to Wilkie, the man running against FDR. Although FDR was losing support because this was his third term he won by a narrow margin.

Knowing what we know of FDR and the coup, we can apply it to today's political spectrum. Nancy Pelosi and the Democrats doing whatever they can to get POTUS expelled from office, lying about Russian collusion, impeachment, the Mueller report, flooding the U.S. with ballots, having a great number of dead people vote and people voting more than once, illegal immigrants voting and scaring senators enough to change their vote about electors. There is nothing more disgusting than people that lie, cheat and steal. Just like Davis and Lewis, Pelosi sold this country out, they did it with Germany, Pelosi did it with China.

The reason POTUS is being harassed is that he can't be controlled. He isn't a politician, he's a businessman that was needed. By running this country like a business we saved billions of dollars. By leaving the Iran deal and Paris Accord alone. The government hacks are going to ruin his life and now you know that if you don't step in line they can do it to you as well. This is the politics the people on the left voted for and I hope that their eyes open after the 29% tax hike and people start losing more jobs than they can cope with on the government level. Obama/Biden had 8 years to fix things and the unemployment level never dropped below 7% and under Donald Trump it was at 3.6% lowest in 50 years. Then COVID came. Donald Trump did things in a timely manner while being told he should have acted earlier and being called a xenophobe for shutting down flights from China and Europe. Some say that it is racist to say the China Virus but that's where it came from. M.E.R.S. came from the Middle East, that's why it's the Middle Eastern Respiratory Syndrome.

What about the sexual things he said about women? He was never charged or had any allegations of rape. Joe Biden has Tara Reed and allegations following that ordeal and will never be asked about it, not to mention the child sniffing he is constantly doing. So the only conclusion is that a normal human being with an I.Q. above room temperature can actually come up with is that this impeachment is political posturing. The Democrats are afraid he will be president again in 2024 and continue to make the Democrats look like they have no idea how to run a country. Also in 4 years we have not been in a war or any conflict except inside our own government. That is mostly by the Democrats constantly opposing him and denying the American aid in the time of need. Nancy Pelosi in the first stimulus gave the Kennedy Center 40 million dollars. I love art like anyone else but what were the Democrats thinking of, wasn't the people. *On 60 Minutes* on Jan. 11, 2021, Nancy Pelosi said yes, she held it up but scrambled to find a way to blame it on the Republicans. The manner in which this has been handled by the Democrats is not only a way to further divide this country, it also shows how incredibly selfish and self-serving the left really is. It is further my opinion that this gives cause for a third party to be formed to keep checks and balances accurate and tri-partisan. This way no one party can hold all 3 branches of government at the same time and it forces debates to come to a ready solution at a quicker pace. This will ensure that the American people are heard and it will restore faith in the government, the Supreme Court and in Congress that we are as a people being heard. Right now the people feel as if no one cares. The people want to be assured that the American business is being conducted with, by and for the American people and the people alone. The people in high positions of office work for us, and we should have a say in every aspect of government business. With China being so close the people want to know why and what they are doing, what are they up to. No one will tell us because they have our new administration in their pocket.

What happens in the next 2 years is gonna be crucial. I am going to make a prediction. We will end up back in the Iran deal and Paris Accord. Biden will get back with NATO, these 3 things alone will cost us billions. Then he will get rid of fracking and start moving away from fossil fuels to go green. Biden says he can create 11 million jobs by pulling away from these. The math doesn't work. He may create 11 million jobs but the American people will lose almost 30 million jobs. Suicide, child abuse and domestic violence will go up exponentially. Crime will go up 20% and the unemployment rate will be at an all-time high. As of Nov. 2020, according to the *Washington Post* homicides were up 28% over the last 9 months. Robbery and rape took a down trend during the same period. Domestic violence homicides through Oct. 8, 2020, are equal to the total of

2018 and 2019 combined according to the BMJ. Child abuse reports have been pervasive and doctors think that lesser injuries are going unreported but the percentage is 5-10 percent higher with parents who lost employment during the pandemic, the actual numbers are elusive because of the lack of reporting. So I'm thinking these crimes will rise considering the trends.

What I think doesn't matter, if it did then my vote would have counted. My son-in-law, my former paramour, her husband, their kids and about 40 friends in their state voted and their votes didn't count. That state has a computer program you log in and it shows your vote, the date you voted and that it was accepted. Every time any of them logged on, it said no record. How is that possible when they had the receipt? This is the reason no one has faith in the election process, especially when the states get flooded with over a million ballots. There was more than one state that had more votes than registered voters. That's why there is no confidence in anything the government does. There is one caveat, though, the Democrats have total control and have no Republicans to blame if something goes awry. 74 million disenfranchised Americans will be watching. CLOSELY.

In order for this administration to run smoothly Biden will have to gain the trust of Trump supporters. I honestly don't think it is possible considering Hillary Clinton called them deplorables and CNN called them hillbilly rubes and so on. None of this is good and we should all strive to be better especially people in positions of power, and the ones tasked to bring the actual news and not hyperbole, rhetoric and incoherent babbling telling people things that they know are not true. The American people are smart independent thinkers. Whereas the Democrats want robots that work for them, and not for themselves.

Socialized medical care and an increase in the welfare system is just another way for the government to be in control. It's called socialism and if it hasn't worked in any country ever I don't understand how people think it will work here and now. It didn't work for Marx, Stalin, Hitler, Mussolini or any Czar or king anywhere. Capitalism is the American way. It won't pay to own a business during the Biden administration as I look at his new tax plan.

Biden wants to tax all who earn 400,000 or more and not the people who make less. The problem with that is it's impossible without the people losing.

How it works is, you tax a company that earns a lot of money, they raise the price of their product and if they still don't meet their bottom line they start laying people off or find reasons to let them go. Companies are in the business to make money and if their profit margin starts to shrink they do what is necessary to make the company profitable. This is why you will see an increase in food, gas, utilities and other things. If the demand for a necessity outweighs the product you see an increase in price. When the product outweighs the demand the price goes down, but if the value of the dollar goes down because of overprinting money or currency change, i.e. gold standard to oil standard or the other way around, the value drops for a short period. If the economy doesn't make a major recovery, our currency will lose its value as a currency. As the U.S. debt grows our monetary value drops considering China owns most of our debt. If the Chinese Yuan makes its way as the new monetary standard for oil the dollar bill will plummet. Then this country will be in dire straits and will have to get another billionaire businessman to figure it out because the people in our government right now would have no clue. They are capable of yelling, screaming, calling names, impeaching, stealing and spending money. They are great for running up debt but as for getting us at a zero balance is an impossibility for this government.

As for capitalism, we need the jobs in the U.S. first. If Biden starts shipping jobs back to China we won't have them here. More people will be living on the streets and not just in Nancy Pelosi's district of San Francisco. All the border states.

When people come here undocumented it drives down the minimum wage, raises taxes and creates a need for more police. American people lose employment opportunities and then there is the crime factor. There is no reason for anyone to be here undocumented and illegal. There are avenues that people can take like, getting an alien registration card. Work or school visa or having a child here. Learning a second language isn't easy, President Teddy Roosevelt did say that this country has room enough for one flag, the American Flag, and one language, English.

It would make it a lot easier if those legal and illegal immigrants learned English, not all of us speak a different language. If I went to live in a different country I would have to learn the language just to get around. It's common sense, not racism.

The bell ringing about everything being racial has to stop. The racial divide that was started by Obama is trending. Now Biden carries that torch, it's all a lie to keep us fighting amongst each other so we are not paying attention to how they are killing us up on Capitol Hill. So they tell us we have white privilege and our whiteness is bad, or how our police are killing just black people, which in itself is a lie. The FBI crime data sheet says that 25% more white men are being shot or killed by police than the black community. It's all an elaborate game so that they get their agenda passed when no one is looking. While you are busy looking for lions you'll get bit by the snakes.

AOC-Alexandria Ocasio-Cortez put out a video on Jan. 13, 2021. She had the audacity to tell Sen. Cruz (R) Tx. and Sen. Josh Hawley (R) Mo. to "get out" after discussions of Biden's illegitimate president conformation. Saying that the Republicans tried to hijack the election. It was the Democrats that for four years had stated that the Trump presidency was illegitimate and that he stole it from Hilary Clinton. She stated that Cruz and Hawley had no proof and that's why Biden won in this fair election. No rebuttal from either senator. My opinion is she should go back to bartending and mopping floors because she is not a proper fit for Congress. When a Congresswoman talks like that and says things no statesman should ever say. I believe she should be censured and relieved of her official capacity in Congress for congressional misconduct.

Now the Democrats are coming for the Constitution and our rights, specifically the First Amendment. Suppression of fundamental rights is just wrong.

The First Amendment bandits strike. Twitter kicked 70,000 people off, as a result of backlash from some of these people saying kicking Trump off of Twitter was wrong. Ironically anyone who had anything pro-Trump on any social media was banned. An agent from AIG insurance in Arizona was kicked off all social media and now has basically no insurance company left. This is how he found clients.

Twitter also came out crying like a 6-year-old with a skinned knee when the president of Uganda banned all social media until after the Ugandan election. Twitter came out with a Tweet saying that no one should be banned from social media because they believe in people's right to speak and be heard. Twitter thought it was unfair. Apparently it hurt Twitter's feelings. The

Ugandan government ordered that all internet services be shut down in Uganda until further notice.

In light of the internet war right now and how much of leftwing big-tech oligarch Democrat dingbats they are, it is understandable why Uganda would take this measure. It's fair and it is the right thing to do.

The Declaration of Independence
IN CONGRESS, July 4, 1776.

The unanimous Declaration of the thirteen united States of America,

When in the Course of human events, it becomes necessary for one people to dissolve the political bands which have connected them with another, and to assume among the powers of the earth, the separate and equal station to which the Laws of Nature and Nature's God entitle them, a decent respect to the opinions of mankind requires that they should declare the causes which impel them to the separation.

We hold these truths to be self-evident, that all men are created equal, that they are endowed by their Creator with certain unalienable Rights, that among these are Life, Liberty, and the pursuit of Happiness – That to secure these rights, Governments are instituted among Men, deriving their just powers from the consent of the governed, — That whenever and Form of Government becomes destructive of these ends, it is the Right of the People to alter or abolish it, and to institute new Government, laying it's foundation on such principles and organizing its powers in such a form, as to them shall seem most likely to effect their Safety and Happiness. Prudence, indeed, will dictate that Governments long established should not be changed for light and transient causes; and accordingly, will experience hath shewn, that mankind are more disposed to suffer, while evils are sufferable, than to right themselves by abolishing forms to which they are accustomed. But when a long train of abuses and usurpations, pursuing invariably the same Object envinces a design to reduce them under absolute Despotism, it is their right, it is their duty, to throw off such Government, and to provide new Guards for their future security. –Such has been the patient sufferance of these Colonies; and such is now the necessity which constrains them to alter their former Systems of Government. The history of the present King of Great Britain is a history of repeated injuries and usurpations, all having in direct object the establishment of an absolute Tyranny over these States. To prove this, let Facts be submitted to a candid world.

He has refused to Assent to Laws, the most wholesome and necessary for the public good.

He has forbidden his Governors to pass Laws of immediate and pressing importance, unless suspended in their operation till his Assent should be obtained; and when so suspended, he has utterly neglected to attend to them.

He has refused to pass other Laws for the accommodation of large districts of people, unless those people would relinquish the right of Representation in the Legislature, a right inestimable to them and formidable to tyrants only.

He has called together legislative bodies at places unusual, uncomfortable, and distant from the depository of their public Records, for the sole purpose of fatiguing them into compliance with his measures.

He has dissolved Representative Houses repeatedly, for opposing with manly firmness his invasions on the rights of the people.

He has refused for a long time, after such dissolutions, to cause others to be elected; whereby the Legislative powers, incapable of Annihilation, have returned to the People at large for their exercise; the State remaining in the meantime exposed to all the dangers of invasion from without, and convulsions within.

He has endeavored to prevent the population of these States; for that purpose obstructing the Laws for Naturalization of Foreigners; refusing to pass others to encourage their migrations hither, and raising conditions of new Appropriations of Lands.

He has obstructed the Administration of Justice, by refusing his Assent to Laws for establishing Judiciary powers.

He has made Judges dependent on his Will alone, for the tenure of their offices, and the amount and payment of their salaries.

He has erected a multitude of New Offices, and sent hither swarms of Officers to harass out people, and eat out their substance.

He has kept among us, in times of peace, Standing Armies without the Consent of our legislatures.

He has affected to render the Military independent of and superior to the Civil power.

He has combined with other to subject us to a jurisdiction foreign to our constitution, and unacknowledged by our laws; giving his Assent to their

Acts of pretended Legislation:

For Quartering large bodies of armed troops among us:

For protecting them, by a mock Trial, from punishment for any Murders which they should commit on the Inhabitants of these states:

For cutting off out Trade with all parts of the world:

For imposing Taxes on us without our consent:

For depriving us in many cases, of the benefits of Trial by Jury:

For transporting us beyond Seas to be tried for pretended offences

For abolishing the free System of English Laws in a neighboring Province, establishing therein an Arbitrary government, and enlarging Boundaries so as to render it at once an example and fit instrument for introducing the same absolute rule into these Colonies:

For taking away our Charters, abolishing our most valuable Laws, and altering fundamentally the Forms of our Governments:

For suspending our own Legislatures, and declaring themselves invested with power to legislate for us in all cases whatsoever.

He has abdicated Government here, by declaring us out of his Protection and waging War against us.

He has plundered our seas, ravaged our Coasts, burnt our towns, and destroyed the lives of our people.

He is at this time transporting large Armies of foreign Mercenaries to complete the works of death, desolation and tyranny, already begun with circumstances of Cruelty & perfidy scarcely paralleled in the most barbarous ages, and totally unworthy the Head of a civilized nation.

He has constrained out fellow Citizens taken Captive on the high Seas to bear Arms against their country, to become the executioners of their friends and Brethren, or to fall themselves by their Hands.

He has excited domestic insurrections amongst us, and has endeavored to bring on the inhabitants of our frontiers, the merciless Indian Savages, whose known rule of warfare, is an undistinguished destruction of all ages, sexes and conditions.

In every stage of these Oppressions, we have Petitioned for Redress in the most humble terms: Our repeated Petitions have been answered only by repeated injury. A Prince whose character is thus marked by every act which may define a Tyrant, is unfit to be the ruler of a free people.

Nor have We been wanting in attentions to our British brethren. We have warned them from time to time of attempts by their legislature to extend an unwarrantable jurisdiction over us. We have reminded them of the circumstances of our emigration and settlement hear. We have appealed to their native justice and magnanimity, and we have conjured them by the ties of our common kindred to disavow these usurpations, which, would inevitably interrupt our connections and correspondence. They too have been deaf to the voice of justice and consanguinity. We must, therefore, acquiesce in the necessity, which denounces our Separation, and hold them, as we hold the rest of mankind, Enemies in War, in Peace Friends.

We, therefore, the Representatives of the unites States of America, in General Congress, Assembled, appealing to the Supreme Judge of the world for the rectitude of out intention, do, in the Name, and by Authority of the good People of these Colonies, solemnly publish and declare, that these United Colonies are, and of Right out to be Free and Independent States; that they are Absolved from all Allegiance to the British Crown, and that all political connection between them and the State of Great Britain, is and ought to be totally dissolved; and that as Free and Independent States, they have full Power to levy War, conclude Peace, contract Alliances, establish Commerce, and to do all other Acts and Things which Independent States may of right do. And for the support of this Declaration, with a firm reliance on the protection of divine Providence, we mutually pledge to each other our Lives, our Fortunes and our sacred Honor.

www.ingramcontent.com/pod-product-compliance
Lightning Source LLC
Chambersburg PA
CBHW070106260726
48658CB00002B/1003